Indian and Free

The publication of this book
was assisted by
The St. Paul Companies, Inc.

INDIAN AND FREE

A Contemporary Portrait of Life
on a Chippewa Reservation

Text and Photographs

by CHARLES BRILL

UNIVERSITY OF MINNESOTA PRESS ☐ MINNEAPOLIS

Published in the United Kingdom and India
by the Oxford University Press,
London and Delhi, and in Canada
by Burns & MacEachern
Ltd., Don Mills, Ontario

Library of Congress Catalog Card Number: 73-91450

ISBN 0-8166-0710-9

This book is dedicated
to the people of Red Lake.

———————

From the beginning I have never
thought of it as my book,
but as our book.

CONTENTS

Prologue

"If you ever saw this place really well, I'm sure you would love Red Lake. It is a place where you could be free as a bird. You could enjoy the beautiful things any time you want to. You could go for walks in the woods, go fishing, go hunting, and go swimming in the lake. I am proud to be a Chippewa Indian."

Alberta Lussier
Grade 8, St. Mary's Mission
School, 1973

"Red Lake, the home of the Indian, is where I was born and it is here that I wish to die."

Donna Cobenais
Grade 7, St. Mary's Mission
School, 1973

PROLOGUE

It was in 1964 that I first visited the Red Lake Indian Reservation in northern Minnesota. I was a staff photographer for the *Minneapolis Tribune* and my assignment was to take pictures of the traditional Fourth of July powwow. There I met, among others, Roger Jourdain, chairman of the Tribal Council, and medicine man Dan Raincloud, with both of whom I formed strong and lasting friendships. I went back to Red Lake as often as I could even after I moved to Ohio to teach at Kent State University. During 1969–1970 (with a grant from the National Endowment for the Humanities) I lived and worked on the reservation, taking thousands of photographs — and also setting nets, hauling fish, carrying traps, and cutting holes through the ice in −20° weather; assisting the teachers in the schools; helping out, whenever possible, in many little ways; sharing, so far as I could, the life on the reservation. I returned in succeeding summers and in the winter of 1972–1973 to renew friendships and to photograph changing ways.

With the approval of the Tribal Council one hundred of my photographs taken during the years 1964–1969 were exhibited in the United States and Canada under the title "Portrait of the Chippewa." The response to the exhibit and the interest shown by the staff of the University of Minnesota Press encouraged me to think of a book. I discussed my plans with the Tribal Council and asked for its continued cooperation. I told the members, "I hope it will be a book that a Red Lake father will show to his sons and grandsons and say, 'This is who we are.' And he will be proud." The council gave me its support.

I regard each of the more than 10,000 photographs from which the 160 in this book are drawn as a gift to me by the people of Red Lake. Thanks to their many acts of friendship and through their generosity and willingness to let me share in their daily activities, I have begun to understand the meaning of the words "the Indian way" — at least the Red Lake Indian way. In this same spirit of friendship and as one means of

expressing my gratitude, I have promised that my profits from the book will go to the Red Lake Chippewa Band.

In the decade since 1964 I have seen a sometimes dramatic, sometimes subtle transition in process within the boundaries of the Red Lake Reservation. Landmarks and buildings of earlier eras have been torn down to make way for the construction of new houses. In 1969 I had an opportunity to photograph what may have been the last wake to take place in a home: the pattern of construction of new homes makes it difficult to remove a coffin through the south window in the traditional manner and it is now common to hold wakes in the community center. In the village of Ponemah the old powwow ring where I saw my first powwow has been abandoned for a location next to the new community center. Madeline Benaise, whom I photographed many times as she cut willow sticks on the farm road and wove baskets on the steps of her cabin, died in 1970. Many others of her generation have also died. Allen Kingbird, Sr., no longer pulls his sled along the snow-packed frozen road of the Point to gather a daily supply of wood but lives in a new one-room home and enjoys the comfort of a fuel-burning stove. When I first met Dan Raincloud, he was living in what he now calls "the old place," a small tar-paper cabin without electricity or running water. Today he lives with his wife Madeline in a multi-unit dwelling for senior citizens, worries about making the monthly rent payment, and is concerned with the increasing amount of his phone bill. The transition from the log house and the tar-paper shack to new five- and six-room prefab homes and modern mobile homes is almost complete; and there is an abundance of accompanying hardware — minibikes, snowmobiles, power lawn mowers — characteristic of suburban living that many visitors do not expect to find.

From the beginning I felt an urgency to record what still remained of the old ways. I also wanted to capture on film the daily activities of a people living as they want to live. If there is a theme to this book it is freedom. Obviously the Red Lake Chippewa do not live in any ideal state of freedom. They have customs and rules and laws; they are subject to pressures from man and nature. But because of the unusual status of the reservation they are free in a way few others on this planet can be. The individual there has the option of being "Indian" — of living close to the land, of hunting and fishing when he wishes, of avoiding constraints and commitments. Or he can choose the white man's way, work from eight to five, and enjoy the goods of modern technology. Or he can take elements from both ways in developing his own life-style.

I admire and respect my Red Lake friends. Indeed I frankly envy them. A reader of an early draft of my manuscript commented that I "romanticized" the Indians and my words dehumanized them by avoiding the negative aspects of their life. I am very much aware of so-called "Indian problems" which plague Red Lake as they do other Indian reservations and communities; I am very much aware too that the scourges of contemporary American society like drugs and pollution have also invaded Red Lake. But it is not the intent of this book to analyze such problems or to offer suggestions for solving them. I believe the people of Red Lake are sensitive to their economic and social problems and are fully capable of

finding solutions without my advice. I am convinced that too frequently the pictures and stories from which outsiders form their image of the Indian overemphasize the negative side and fail to promote real understanding. The same reader said that anyone reading my text and then visiting Red Lake for the first time would not recognize it. In a sense that is precisely what I intend: to show the reservation in a light that first-time, casual, or unsympathetic visitors would not see. Travelers to strange lands — and Indian reservations — see only what they have time to see. And some see only what they want to see.

I am not an anthropologist. I am not a historian or political scientist or economist or sociologist. In the text that follows I have tried to provide some background and context for the photographs. I have tried to answer questions readers might have about the Red Lake Indians and their reservation. But I leave to others ethnographic and demographic studies. I report what my eyes have seen, what Red Lakers have told me voluntarily, and a little of what I have read in such basic sources as William W. Warren's *History of the Ojibway Nation* (1853), Frances Densmore's *Chippewa Customs* (1929), Ruth Landes's *Ojibwa Sociology* (1937) and *Ojibwa Religion and the Midewiwin* (1968), Sister M. Inez Hilger's *Chippewa Child Life and Its Cultural Background* (1951), Erwin F. Mittelholtz's *Historical Review of the Red Lake Indian Reservation* (1957), and the Minnesota League of Women Voters' *Indians in Minnesota* (1971).

I have sat on the bow of a fishboat and discussed weekly fish checks and the December fish bonus because that is what the men talk about. And while pulling nets I've been told to count each walleye, and sometimes whitefish, hauled into the boat. Some days the count doesn't pay for the gas; on a good day the tally may reach four or five hundred and the men will joke and say, "Look at that, Charlie, look at that. Today we made lots of money." I have read that the per capita income on the Red Lake Reservation is $1474. But I've never asked a man at Red Lake how much money he makes.

I have been honored by an invitation to eat with the men during the feast before burial ceremonies; many times I have shared in the passing of ceremonial tobacco, and I have been allowed to observe the religious ceremonies and curing rites of the Midewiwin ("Grand Medicine Society"). One Christmas when all the Red Lake men begged off I was elected to put on a Santa suit and beard and pass out gifts to the children. (I wasn't too convincing. As soon as I walked onto the stage of the grade school all my little friends shouted, "Hi, Charlie!")

Last March — all things take place when the time is right — Dan Raincloud in his quiet manner said it was time that I had an Indian name. One evening I brought the traditional gifts of food and tobacco and in a short ceremony Dan became my sponsor: "I choose the bird Kenew — Golden Eagle — to be this man's name and for him to be watched by this bird." Many times I had said to Dan that I wished I were an eagle so that I could soar high above the land and observe everything.

Even if I had the eagle's vision, this book could not show "everything," but I hope it will reveal the richness and meaningfulness of the way of life and something of the spirit of this one group of Americans who are the Red Lake Chippewa Indians.

"Freedom Is Our Heritage"

"This property under discussion, called Red Lake, is my property. These persons whom you see before you are my children. They own this place the same as I own it. My friends, I ask that we reserve the whole of the lake as ours and that of our grandchildren hereafter."

May-dway-gwa-no-nind, head chief
of Red Lake, during the
Seventh Open Council to discuss
the Treaty of 1889

"I remember my father-in-law telling me about one of the last Great Lakes councils of the Chippewa tribes in Duluth in the early 1900s. All the bands, except Red Lake, had ceded their land to the government and accepted individual allotments. Some of the Minnesota Chippewa delegates had actually chartered a train to make the trip. The men wore high top hats and silk shirts, with those high stiff white celluloid collars that button on the shirt. Their women were dressed in the finest fashions with silk. When the delegates from Red Lake arrived the others made fun of them: 'Look at the poor Red Lakers; see how shabbily they dress and appear not to have enough to eat.' Then Baptiste Thunder spoke: 'My friends, you make fun of us. But look at you. You have sold your land and are rich. But you have also sold your jackpine, your Norway pine, and your white pine . . . and your porcupine.' "

Roger Jourdain, chairman,
Red Lake Tribal Council, 1973

"We can go hunting any time of the season and fishing too. Not all people have that privilege. We can do this because we have a closed reservation. If our reservation was open, all or most of our wildlife would die. Red Lake is a closed reservation and I hope it will stay that way."

Allen Branchaud
Grade 7, St. Mary's Mission
School, 1973

"FREEDOM IS OUR HERITAGE"

It is Red Lake's legal status as a "closed reservation" that makes this Chippewa reservation unique in Minnesota. The land of the Red Lake Band was never ceded to the United States government and then set aside as an Indian reservation under federal jurisdiction: the almost universal procedure elsewhere; the members of the band claim possession of the land by right of conquest and aboriginal title. During a century of negotiations over treaties and other agreements between the Chippewa of Minnesota and the United States government, Red Lake leaders from the hereditary chief May-dway-gwa-no-nind (He That Is Spoken To) to Roger Jourdain, the first elected chairman of the Tribal Council, have refused to allow their land to be broken up and part of it sold to non-Indian interests.

As a result the Red Lakers — some 4000 living on the reservation — walk and hunt freely through more than half a million acres of woodlands, fish without hindrance the waters of 210 lakes and numerous streams, govern themselves as a semisovereign nation through the Tribal Council, and maintain a way of life that is specially their own.

The contrast with the other Chippewa reservations in Minnesota is striking. By a series of treaties and federal acts between 1854 and 1889 six "open" reservations were created on which specific allotments were to be made for each individual Indian (it was not until the late 1880s that the allotment policy was extensively implemented). The land remaining after allotment was to be sold by the government and the money used to give the Indians "houses, farming implements, and schools, and to make [them] a happy and prosperous people" (in the words of Bishop Martin Marty during negotiations preceding the Treaty of 1889). As the farmer and lumberman moved in, however, the Indian in many cases was forced to move out. The reservations became checkered with non-Indian-owned tracts. The most blatant examples are Leech Lake and White Earth reservations in northwestern Minnesota where less than

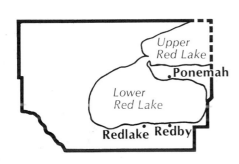

10 percent of each of the original reservations is Indian-owned. As President Grover Cleveland had remarked when he signed the General Allotment Act of 1887, the "hunger and thirst of the white man for the Indian's land is almost equal to his hunger and thirst after righteousness."

The story of the white man's depredations against American Indians as a group is too well known to need repeating here. The story of the Red Lake Reservation, on the other hand, is, I think, little known. For me its motif — in counterpoint to that of recent Indian history generally — is freedom.

Upper and Lower Red Lake, connected by a three-quarter-mile-wide channel called the Narrows, is one of the largest fresh-water lakes wholly within the boundaries of one state. It lies thirty miles north of Bemidji, Minnesota, seventy-five miles east of the North Dakota border, and sixty miles south of the United States–Canada boundary. The Red Lake Reservation almost encircles the 230,000 acres of Upper and Lower Red Lake, stretching west and north. The land area owned by the Red Lake Band (including the Northwest Angle and scattered restored lands which are not contiguous with the reservation) totals 805,722 acres covering 1259 square miles — an area equal in size to the state of Rhode Island. There are 320 miles of roads and trails crossing the wooded acres of the reservation. Highways 1 and 89 are sixty-mile-an-hour north-south and east-west routes through the reservation; sandy wilderness roads like the North Shore Trail are used daily in summer by fishermen, and in winter by loggers. A hundred miles of brush-lined, grass-humped fire and logging trails cross the wooded backcountry, touching spring-fed lakes and circling meadowland. Some (like a twelve-mile trail to the Narrows) are almost forgotten and end at logging camps and Indian villages that have vanished. The "main street" of the reservation is the thirty-five-mile blacktop road that begins at the village of Redlake on the southern edge of Lower Red Lake and follows the shoreline of the lake east through Redby, then north to the Point where Ponemah is located.

Redlake, largest of the three villages, has a population of 1700; Redby has 1100, Ponemah, 700. Ninety percent of the reservation population live in the villages; the rest live in scattered homes.

Fishing and lumbering are economic activities of importance on the reservation.

The money fish of Red Lake is the sweet fish of the lakes, Sis-Kay-Way (walleye pike). Each year more than a half million pounds of pike, perch, and whitefish are taken from the rust-colored waters of Lower and Upper Red Lake. Since commercial fishing began as a tribal profit-sharing cooperative in 1929, the cycle of setting and pulling nets has provided a summer income for many families. Twenty years ago almost half of the families on the reservation fished commercially. Today, the availability of other income opportunities and a few poor seasons have reduced the number to fewer than a hundred families. Many of the summer "fish camps" on the west end in the area of the Sandy and Red Lake rivers are abandoned. The long pointed poles of the net-hanging racks stand barren like winter trees. Today most of the commercial fishing takes place north of Redlake from Mahquam Bay to Ponemah Point. For many of the families in the Ponemah area, fishing continues to be the main income-producing activity from May till mid-November. The Red Lake Fisheries Association has plans to expand and do its own processing. This cooperative has an annual budget of $500,000. Members of the cooperative share in the profits of the operation (through a Christmas bonus) as well as being paid for the fish they catch. The band receives in royalties a percentage of sales.

Commercial timberlands occupy some 330,000 acres. There have been sawmills on the reservation since 1868, although not in continuous operation. The Red Lake Indian Mill at Redby was modernized in 1972 to enable the mill to increase its lumber production from 5 million board feet a year to 9–11 million board feet. The Red Lake Mill has an annual operating budget of $1,247,000. Adjacent to the sawmill are two allied wood-product manufacturing plants: the Red Lake Chippewa Cedar Fence Plant, which turns about 3000 cords of cedar bolt into picket fencing annually, and the Red Lake Pre-Fab Housing Plant. In all these plants, 98 percent of the work force is local.

Early government and missionary reports concerning the reservation stressed the presence of fertile farmland. S. T. Bardwell, agent for the American Missionary Association, wrote in 1851 that "the soil at Red Lake is the best I have ever seen in the territory, and produces abundantly almost all kinds of grain and vegetables." The grain crop in 1868 was reported to be more than 7000 bushels. Today, although the state Department of Forestry lists 4880 acres of the reservation as dry farmland, there are only two commercial farm operations on it. Located on the flat grasslands of the western boundary, they belong to two brothers of the Red Lake Band and are typical of the farms along state highway 1, leading to Thief River Falls. Some families still maintain home gardens, but the once common two- and three-acre plots that produced enough surplus corn and potatoes to save members of other Chippewa bands from starvation during the winter of 1842–1843 are now overgrown with sumac and marked with decayed cedar posts and rusty wire.

Since 1969 the commercial growing of wild rice has become a tribal enterprise. Red Lake has about 300 acres now in production, with an estimated 55,000 acres of land being suitable for cultivation.

There are 480 tribal members employed in federal and tribal positions. Many of these are women. The role of Chippewa women, once limited to maintaining the home and helping harvest and prepare foods, has expanded. Modern technology and changing mores have opened new options for the Red Lake woman, as they have for her white sister. In many homes she provides a second income by working as a secretary, classroom aid, or public health service assistant, or in one of the other federal and tribal positions. Some women work in professional and specialized jobs, such as schoolteachers, dental assistants, practical nurses, and home economists. A Red Lake woman is director of the Headstart Program and recently another woman was named director of the newly created Drug Abuse Center. Two women now serve on the Red

Lake School Board and many have become active in planning and directing activities at the neighborhood community centers. Although it is still the practice for women to dance as a group at powwows in a slow, sedate manner leaving the fancy dancing to the men, they are setting records on the ball field and basketball court: organized women's slow pitch and basketball have become popular spectator sports. Some Red Lake women continue to follow old patterns of the Indian way, but most have modified their life-styles to accommodate things that interest them in the modern world.

In some respects Redlake, Redby, and Ponemah are typical American small towns. It is common to find three generations living within walking distance of each other and sharing common experiences. The older people are respected and cared for by relatives and friends. There is a general store in each town, a gas station, a church; Redlake has a twelve-grade school, Ponemah an elementary school. The residents gather for celebrations and mourning and for "town meetings."

Red Lakers are not isolated from the outside world. I am always amazed when someone asks me, "Can the Indians leave the reservation?" There are no fences around the reservation; the roads to Bemidji and other cities in the area are well traveled. (In the early years of the reservation, Indians did have to get passes from the resident Indian agent whenever they wished to leave; that has not been the case since 1890.) It is common for Red Lakers to drive to larger cities to shop in the supermarkets and discount stores; to bowl with the league on Tuesday and Thursday evenings; to play Bingo at the American Legion Club in Bemidji. Some commute to classes at Bemidji State College. In addition to the *Redlake Neighborhood Centers Newsletter*, published by the Red Lake Tribal Council to inform the community of news and events of local importance, many people subscribe to the *Bemidji Pioneer* and the *Minneapolis Tribune*. Television is popular and reception is generally good.

There are some outward signs of "Indianness" on the reservation. (Neither wigwams nor birchbark canoes are in evidence, however.) As one crosses the boundary line of the reservation on state highway 89 or on the gravel road at Jerome Cutoff or on the sandy North Shore Trail, there is likely to be a sign:

WARNING. THIS IS INDIAN LAND. NO TRESPASSING. NO FISHING, HUNTING, CAMPING, BERRY PICKING, PEDDLING OR SOLICITING WITHOUT AUTHORIZED PERMIT FROM RED LAKE TRIBAL COUNCIL OFFICE. VIOLATORS AND TRESPASSERS WILL BE PROSECUTED UNDER FEDERAL LAW 86-634.

In Ponemah one may hear the soft melodic accents of the Chippewa language as a group of men pause to pass the time of day. During feasts the ceremonial tobacco will be passed. On a summer night the beat of a drum punctuates the stillness beside a lake. Medicine bags hang on the sides of homes in Ponemah to ward off sickness.

But the special Indian quality of the Red Lake Reservation lies more in intangibles. Ask a man why he lives here and one of his reasons will be freedom: a freedom described in various ways. To do what he pleases. To be his own boss if he wants to work in the woods or set nets. To exchange of a morning small talk with a friend whenever he's so inclined. Some say it is a freedom from the white man's way of thinking. On many occasions while we were discussing some local issue, Roger Jourdain would wave a pointed finger in my direction and say, "That's the trouble; you're thinking like a white man." In time I began to understand that it comes down to a question of priorities. What is of the greatest importance to the white man may simply not fall within the Red Laker's range of values and interests and he will ignore it.

It must be stressed that the Indian way of Red Lakers is of course not that of their seventeenth-century forebears, nor is their freedom of the same character. Outsiders like myself may regret some of the intrusions of the modern world into the everyday life of the reservation. We may find it paradoxical that the children write lyrically of the joys of Red Lake while so many of their elders leave the reservation or bring onto it white-inspired ways and things that seem incongruous. But the Red Lakers are making their own choices, setting their own priorities, molding their life-styles to suit themselves. They are not totally free; no one is. They are not always consistent; they see no reason to be.

It seems to me that the attitudes of the Red Lakers — their spirit if I may so term it — stem from a strong bond with nature, the land, and with each other, from a sense of personal dignity and worth which they have never lost, and from a lively awareness of their long tradition and history. Many times while photographing the children playing on the sandy beaches and running through the shallow waters on the west end, I have been reminded that here, at the mouth of the Big Sandy River, on a summer day two hundred years ago, a band of Red Lake warriors fought a bloody encounter with a Sioux war party. The Red Lake Chippewa have lived on the shores of this lake since the early 1700s and many, especially in the Ponemah area, can trace their ancestry to the great chiefs and warriors who held council on the banks of the Blackduck and Battle rivers. Let me sketch a little of the traditional-historical background that is so important to these people.

The Chippewa or Ojibway (Ojibwa) Indians form one of the principal branches of the Algonquian family of aboriginal North Americans. "Chippewa" and "Ojibway" both refer to the same tribe of Indians (more than seventy other names have been applied to the tribe as well, according to ethnologist Sister M. Inez Hilger, among them Achipoes, Uchipgouin, Dewakanha, Dshipewehaga, Ninniwas, and Saulteaux). I believe "Ojibway" is what the Red Lakers themselves generally prefer (they also call themselves "Anishinabe," first man or original man), "Chippewa" being a corruption or anglicization of "Ojibway." "Chippewa," however, is the designation found in most treaties and is most common in popular parlance; and somewhat reluctantly I have decided to use the familiar term in this book.

The derivation of "Ojibway (Chippewa)" has occasioned speculation among those interested in language, but the explanations offered are perhaps more ingenious than convincing to linguists. According to William W. Warren in his *History of the Ojibway Nation*, "Ojibway" is composed of two Indian words, "O-jib," meaning to pucker up, and "ub-way," meaning to roast. Warren suggests how the name came to be applied to the tribe. These people, he says, were "accustomed to secure captives, whom under the uncontrolled feeling incited by aggravated wrong, and revenge for similar injuries, they tortured by fire in various ways. The name of Ab-boin-ug (roasters), which the Ojibways have given to the Dahcotas or Sioux, originated in their roasting their captives, and it is as likely that the word Ojibwa (to roast till puckered up), originated in the same manner." (Another possibility Warren mentions is that the name comes from a characteristic of a moccasin they wore, which had a lengthwise puckered seam.)

Warren, born in 1825, son of a Chippewa woman and a white man, also records the legendary beginnings of the tribe as related to him by an old priest. (Warren comments, "The belief of the Algics [Algonquians] is . . . that they are a spontaneous people. They do not pretend, as a people, to give any reliable account of their first creation. It is a subject which to them is buried in darkness and mystery.")

"Our forefathers," the priest told Warren, "many string of lives ago, lived on the shores of the Great Salt Water in the east. Here it was, that while congregated in a great town, and while they were suffering the ravages of sickness and death, the Great Spirit, at the intercession of Man-ab-o-sho, the great common uncle of the An-ish-in-aub-ag, granted them this rite wherewith life is restored and prolonged. Our forefathers moved from the shores of the great water, and proceeded westward. The Me-da-we lodge [the lodge of the "Grand Medicine Society," where the rite was performed] was pulled down and it was not again erected, till our forefathers again took a stand on the shores of the great river near where Mo-ne-aung (Montreal) now stands.

"In the course of time this town was again deserted, and our forefathers still proceeding westward, lit not their fires till they reached the shores of Lake Huron, where again the rites of Me-da-we were practised.

"Again these rites were forgotten, and the Me-da-we lodge was not built till the Ojibways found themselves congregated at Bow-e-ting (outlet of Lake Superior [Sault Ste. Marie]), where it remained for many winters. Still the Ojibways moved westward, and for the last time the Me-da-we lodge was erected on the Island of La Pointe, and here, long before the pale face appeared among them, it was practised in its purest and most original form. Many of our fathers lived the full term of life granted to mankind by the Great Spirit, and the forms of many old people were mingled with each rising generation."

According to Warren the Chippewa first collected in one central village at La Pointe in the year 1490 and were first visited by the white man about 1612.

From the time the Chippewa left Sault Ste. Marie their western advance was marked by frequent and bloody encounters with the Sioux and Fox who occupied the country bordering Lake Superior. The island of La Pointe was selected for their main village because it provided natural protection from bands of Sioux war parties. When the French fur traders Chouart and Radisson visited the central part of what is now Minnesota in 1659–1660 only hunting and raiding parties of the Chippewa had penetrated the area. As the main tribes of Chippewa moved slowly into the rice lakes of Wisconsin and the hunting grounds of Minnesota they pushed the Sioux out — considerably aided by the firearms they received from the French. By the early 1700s bands of Chippewa were found living as far north as Rainy Lake on the Canadian-Minnesota border and as far west as Red Lake in Minnesota.

"In 1737, the Sioux sent a party of thirty warriors to the vicinity of Lake Superior which resulted in the killing of an Ojibwa family. From this time on the Ojibwa began a relentless march against the Sioux in central and northern Minnesota which lasted nearly a century. . . . [In 1765] the Sioux withdrew from the Red Lake area after a bloody encounter with the Chippewas (Ojibwa) near the mouth of the Sandy River [located at the west end of the Red Lake Reservation] around Big Stone in which Cross Lake (Ponemah) Indians annihilated the entire Sioux party. The Sioux previously had laid in ambush and killed one Chippewa trapper and wounded another near the mouth of the Battle River [which crosses the road to Ponemah] and had fled." So did one historian, Erwin F. Mittelholtz, describe some of the early Indian-against-Indian conflict in the region. When David Thompson, geographer for the Northwest Company of Montreal, reached Red Lake in 1798 he found an old chief, She-she-she-pus-kut, and six lodges of Indians. In succeeding decades explorers, traders, and missionaries moved through the area or stayed for a time, making only tantalizingly brief records. The government in Washington had its representatives on the scene early. In 1869 the Indian agent, Captain Hassler, noted: "I cannot speak too highly of the conduct of these Indians since I have had charge of this agency. They are a sober, industrious, and well behaved tribe."

July 6, 1889, stands as perhaps the most important date in the history of the Red Lake Chippewa Band. This was the occasion of the signing of the Treaty of 1889, climaxing the last of the great councils between hereditary Indian chiefs and commissioners of the United States government. The agreement of 1889 represents a "Declaration of Independence" for the Red Lake Band, an "Indian victory," in that the Chippewa leaders steadfastly refused to accede to the government's allotment plan and — against all odds — maintained the integrity of their reservation.

The spokesman of the commissioners addressed the Red Lake representatives: "Will you go backward or will you go forward and see, in the future, your children happy and prosperous, able to care for you in your old age, and with horses and cattle and wagons and mills — every thing that civilization will bring you? So, with only blackness, sorrow and distress on the one hand, you may on the other hand go upward in the bright sunlight of future prosperity. You occupy today a position in which you are to choose whether you go down or whether you rise to a better life. You must not forget that the President acts toward you with all the light that civilization has given him. He knows that in order to become self-supporting, to till the ground and raise such things as you need as civilized people, you must be assisted and guided, and he is willing to assist and guide you to prosperity."

The means by which the Indians were to be guided to prosperity and civilization was cession of their land to "the great white father," which land would then be allotted to permit individual ownership of property, regarded by the white man, in the words of a commissioner, as "one of the most effective civilizing agencies."

The Red Lake leaders did not find the argument persuasive: they had observed acutely the less-than-advantageous results of early cessions and allotments. Nah-gaun-e-gwon-abe (Leading Feather) noted that the Indian "has ceded a vast number of acres; enough to raise a large number of American people upon. What have we to mark these cessions? See the cessions the Red Lake Indians have made. See the amount of land thus populated by the whites and number of children born there — even on the comparatively little land we have ourselves ceded. Look now at the condition we are in. What do we get for all the cessions we have made? See the prosperity of those who have benefited by the cessions we have made. Look at the dilapidated condition of those people here. This shows why we have been so slow in coming to an agreement."

May-dway-gwa-no-nind, then in his eighties, spoke: "I am getting aged; I see that I shall be called upon by the Master of Life to deliver an account of myself. . . . I must look to my grandchildren and their children's grandchildren; I must look after the benefit of all. . . . This property under discussion, called Red Lake, is my property. These persons whom you see before you are my children. They own this place the same as I own it. My friends, I ask that we reserve the whole of the lake as ours and that of our grandchildren hereafter." Later he added: "We wish to guarantee to our posterity some security; that is why we demand the reservation we have outlined on that paper. It is not greediness that influences us. This tribe is growing year by year, and we think it is our duty to protect those that come after us. We know the character of our country here. There are only meadows in certain places; there are trees we would get our fuel from. All these things do not grow together, so the tract must be made larger so as to combine all the things we want. We want the reservation we now select to last ourselves and our children forever. I shall touch the pen with the understanding that all you have said to us is the truth; that you respect the truth and the words of our Great Father. And in the mean time we want you to remember the occasion that has made us stand here, pleading for the future."

Agreement was at length reached. In return for cession of some lands the Red Lake Band was to receive $90,000 annually for fifty years, plus interest on money received for the sale of ceded land. But the central reservation was preserved intact and withstood challenges over the years, the latest one being turned back in federal courts nearly a half century after May-dway-gwa-no-nind, Nah-gaun-e-gwon-abe, and 151 others of the Red Lake Band affixed their marks to the Treaty of 1889. In 1934–1935 when the Red Lakers rejected the Indian Reorganization Act and asserted their independence from the Minnesota Chippewa Tribe, they were upheld by the Court of Claims, which ruled that the Red Lake Band of Chippewa Indians was the sole and exclusive owner of the Red Lake Reservation, a judgment affirmed by the Supreme Court.

During the last half century, two men have assumed the position of leader and spokesman for the Red Lake Chippewa Band — Peter Graves and Roger Jourdain. Both men have fought to protect the heritage of the Red Lake people. Peter Graves successfully organized the General Council of the Red Lake Band in 1918 and held the position of secretary-treasurer until his death in 1957. In 1918 the Red Lake chiefs decided to document their authority as the legal council of the tribe with a written constitution — and became the first chiefs among the Minnesota Chippewa bands to adopt such a document. The 1918 constitution provided for a council consisting of seven chiefs and five appointees by each chief. This system of representation followed a pattern that had long characterized the band. In the early years a chief and a group of followers would from time to time move out to settle a new area — Cross Lake (later Ponemah), Battle River, Redby. To discuss common problems, the chiefs would meet and form a council.

Roger Jourdain, born on the reservation in a log house at Little Rock and educated in Indian boarding schools, has been the chairman of the Tribal Council for fifteen years. Most people use at least one of the following words when describing him: tough, smart, politician. He's a fighter and can challenge a proposal with an amazing ability to recall Chippewa history and cite contracts and agreements that were not in the best interest of the Red Lake Band. He was one of the band members who advocated a reform of the 1918 constitution to replace the traditional leadership of hereditary chiefs with popular elections. In 1958 a revision of the constitution was approved and the first election took place. Today elections are held every four years. The council chairman, treasurer, and secretary are elected at large; two councilmen are elected from each of four districts. All enrolled members of the band who are twenty-five or older may vote. Referendum and recall are provided for. Amendments to the constitution may be passed by a majority vote provided 25 percent of the qualified electorate have voted in the election.

The Tribal Council has both governmental and business authority which includes the right to represent the band in negotiations with other agencies of government and private persons, to regulate and license business activities within the reservation, to remove intruders, to enact law and order ordinances, to maintain a police force and tribal court, and to regulate inheritance. (In 1953 when the state of Minnesota was given civil and criminal authority over Indian reservations Red Lake was exempt. At Red Lake there is a federal Indian police force, operating under a tribal code of Indian offenses; a Court of Indian Offenses handles civil and minor criminal cases when only Indians are involved. Major crimes and any Indian crime against a non-Indian, unless tribal law covers its punishment, are matters for the federal courts.)

The council is authorized to administer funds within control of the band, prepare budget requests for funds deposited in the

United States Treasury to the band's credit, lease tribal lands and resources, and set rules and regulations for fishing and hunting by nonmembers of the band. Nonmembers may obtain fishing and hunting permits on a daily or seasonal basis. Any married members over twenty-one, or younger with special approval, may apply for a land-use permit. A 1961 tribal ordinance limits land allocations to a five-acre homesite and three lots within city limits. Permits for agricultural use are limited to 320 acres but often depend on location and availability of land. With tribal permission and review nonmembers can obtain a renewable lease to operate a store or other commercial business within the reservation. In recent years the Tribal Council has authorized some twenty business and agricultural leases on tribal lands.

Over the years the Tribal Council has enforced a policy prohibiting the sale of liquor on the reservation, although there is no restriction on the bringing of liquor onto the reservation. Again and again I have heard the inevitable query, often asked in a sympathetic tone and delicately worded, about Indians and their drinking habits. Briefly stated: Yes, the Chippewa drink and have since the early days of the fur trade when the English traders offered six quarts of West Indian rum for one beaver pelt and the French bartered with brandy. They sometimes drink a good deal. As a young friend of mine joked, "Well, Charlie, the white man stops off every night for a drink; we don't have any bars here, so we save it all for the weekend." Drinking at Red Lake — generally a spontaneous gathering of neighbors around a couple of cases of beer — is done with equal amounts of enthusiasm and sociability. The accompanying conversation is light, seldom controversial, with much joking and storytelling, usually in Chippewa. If the mood is appropriate and a drum handy, the men will sing.

The problems related to drinking in our society are also apparent within the boundaries of the reservation. Alcoholism has been given as a reason for the high incidence of traffic deaths on the reservation. It should be noted, however, that the reservation is a rural area, and in rural areas people are more apt to drive longer distances at greater speeds. For example, it is common for a Red Lake resident to drive the sixty-mile roundtrip to Bemidji on an evening's outing — and through snowdrifts and subzero winds that would close schools and cancel events in other parts of the country. There is an awareness among Red Lakers of the problems drinking may lead to, and for those who wish it, medical help is available on the reservation through the services of the United States Department of Health, Education, and Welfare.

Because of Red Lake's unique status as a closed reservation the United States Bureau of Indian Affairs works there under the Tribal Council as a participating, not a governing, agency. Royce Graves, council secretary, defined the role of the BIA as one of "protecting the interest of the band, not taking care of the people." Its main function is to act as a liaison between the Tribal Council and the federal government.

The Tribal Council working with the BIA has seen the accomplishment of civic improvements. Since 1960 a tribal housing

Roger Jourdain, chairman of the Red Lake Tribal Council

program (with funding from federal agencies such as the Department of Housing and Urban Development, the Farmers Home Administration, and the Veterans Administration) has brought about much-needed housing construction. Presently standard homes number about 350 with some 60 "transition" dwellings (mostly mobile units) in addition; there is need for 300 more new homes. A new vocational school has been completed at Redlake, a new fire station and office building at Ponemah; and construction has begun on a new one-million-dollar Law and Order Center at Redlake.

The Tribal Council and the BIA have also cooperated in supervising the activities of certain federal agencies and programs seeking to help the Red Lakers carry out their responsibilities and meet some of their problems. The most notable perhaps have been the programs of Comprehensive Health Services and Project Headstart, both operating under the Department of Health, Education, and Welfare.

Red Lakers receive direct free health care under the Comprehensive Health Services program. Doctors, nurses, and dentists provide free medical services on the reservation, and cases may be referred to outside specialists or to hospitals in Bemidji, Grand Forks, and Minneapolis. Several Red Lake women have been trained to work as home aides, to give personal care under supervision, and to assist with housekeeping services in the home. The Public Health Service hospital at Red Lake has a staff of sixty-seven, including fifty-three tribal members.

This free health care is one of the few financial benefits accruing to the Red Lakers *as Indians*. Contrary to what I have found to be a widespread assumption, neither Red Lakers nor other Indians, whether they live on a reservation or not, receive individual financial support from the federal government just because they are Indians. Like non-Indians they may get welfare or social security benefits. Occasionally tribal members do share moneys paid by the United States to settle claims against the government for unjust land dealings. In 1964 as a result of such a claim each member of the Red Lake Band received $200. Although Indians living on the reservation do not pay property taxes, they must pay all other taxes to which their nonreservation activities subject them.

Project Headstart, a preschool program for children three to five years, has been a highly regarded and successful program. The classes are under the direction of the women and young adults of the community. In 1970–1971, 160 children were enrolled at Red Lake.

The earliest record of an educational institution conducted for the benefit of the Red Lake Indians was a mission school opened in 1843 by the American Missionary Association. By 1877 when the community of Redlake had a population of 1000 the government had built the first Indian boarding school. In 1889 two Roman Catholic priests and two sisters arrived and opened a boarding school in the old American Company fur-trading post. That same year they were given land by the Tribal Council and established St. Mary's Mission, including a larger boarding school. The public school system was established in 1935. In 1937 there were 100 students enrolled in the Redlake public school, grades 1 to 12.

Today Red Lake is an Independent School District in the state system. There are modern school buildings and classrooms and a fully accredited program. The curriculum is up to date and offers both college preparatory and vocational programs. The school board consists of Red Lake Band members and works closely with the Red Lake superintendent of schools in establishing school policy.

The 1972 school census listed 1862 students under twenty years of age: 953 boys and 908 girls; of these 194 attended St. Mary's Mission School, the rest the public schools at Redlake and Ponemah. In Ponemah the elementary school includes kindergarten to sixth grade. After grade 6 the students are bused to Redlake.

A student transferring from another school system would find the transition normal. The courses are similar and extracurricular activities — band, sports, and clubs — are marked by an enthusiastic school spirit. Where the curriculum permits there is a natural emphasis on Indian culture: art, history, literature. The library facility is excellent and has a fine collection of Indian literature. There are some Indian teachers in the elementary and vocational schools and as positions are vacated an active effort is made to recruit qualified Indian teachers.

In 1960 there were fourteen high school graduates from Redlake school; in 1973 there were thirty-two. Between 90 and 95 percent of the graduating seniors now enter college or technical-vocational schools. The availability of BIA financial aids, state school Indian grants, and Office of Equal Opportunity grants has in recent years given any qualified Indian student the opportunity to go on to advanced education. The proximity of Bemidji State College, which has developed an excellent liberal arts program, has made it possible for many Red Lake young people and adults to attend college classes and live at home. The college offers coursework in American Indian studies and gives language courses in beginning, intermediate, and advanced Chippewa.

This, then, is the Red Lake Reservation — admittedly as seen from one man's point of view; it is a picture shaped by my personal interests, reflecting the inevitable limitations of the written word which can convey little enough of the vitality of these people or the beauties of water and woods they live so close to.

In the pages to come, my photographs will, I hope, speak more tellingly for me — and of the Red Lake Reservation.

"I like Red Lake because everything is so free. It is warm in the summer, but cold in the winter. In the summer we can go picking wild berries. We have a powwow. It is a time when we get together and dance Indian.

"If I had to leave I would run and hide because in the cities there is too much noise and in Red Lake it is peaceful; all you can hear is the lovely sounds of the birds singing. In the cities there is too much

traffic. Up here in Red Lake there is just a little bit of traffic.

"In Red Lake we have our own police station, hospitals and fire house, and a free dentist. In Red Lake all our animals are free to roam the woods while many other places put them in cages. I like Red Lake just because it is Red Lake."

Sherry Garrigan
Grade 6, St. Mary's Mission
School, 1973

"Why I Like It Here:

1. the woods
2. the lake
3. the wildlife
4. the hospital
5. the doctors
6. our law
7. our fish
8. our family
9. our dentists
10. our teachers"

Helen Sayers
Grade 5, St. Mary's Mission
School, 1973

Faces of the People

"In their continual effervescence of animal spirits, open-heartedness, and joviality, [the French voyageurs] agreed fully with the like characteristics possessed by the Ojibways. Some of my readers may be surprised at my thus placing the Indian on a par with the laughter-loving Frenchman, for the reason that he has ever been represented as a morose, silent, and uncommunicative being. It is only necessary to state that this is a gross mistake, and but a character (far different from his real one), assumed by the Indian in the presence of strangers, and especially white strangers in whom he has no confidence."

William W. Warren, in
History of the Ojibway Nation, 1853

"There are none here who are owned by anyone; each one owns himself and is master of his own ideas."

Pus-se-nous (Slapping Off Flies),
speaking at the Third Council of 1889

FACES OF THE PEOPLE

On March 22, 1972, Anna Garrigan, sitting at the kitchen table of her house trailer, tapped her pencil, looked at the ceiling, and announced: "There are 6000 members on the Red Lake Band roll." Mrs. Garrigan was still in the process of adding and subtracting but was close enough to call this "a pretty accurate figure." She had spent most of the winter scanning the pages of the tribal roll to bring enrollment figures up to date.

Today two-thirds of the enrolled members — 625 families — live on the reservation; many of the 2000 individuals who live off the reservation have moved to the Twin Cities of St. Paul and Minneapolis. (There are 23,000 Indians in the state of Minnesota; approximately a third live in the Twin Cities.)

The tribal roll is the official record of Red Lake Chippewa Band membership. Upon the pages of this heavy, leather-bound ledger with its neat entries the members of each family are recorded alphabetically next to the names of parents and grandparents, with dates of birth and death, and degree of Red Lake Chippewa blood. In order to qualify for the privileges of membership one must have a minimum of one-fourth Red Lake Indian blood and be duly enrolled as a member of the band. The precursor of the present tribal roll was a census conducted in 1889 in order to fulfill one of the provisions of the treaty of that year which required a two-thirds vote of the male Indians over eighteen before the treaty took effect. The census listed 1168 Red Lake and Pembina Band Chippewa males on the land from Red Lake to the Canadian border and west to the Dakotas.

After the Red Lake Band organized under a written constitution in 1918 it was agreed that all Indians born on the reservation would be given membership. Roger Jourdain has recalled those early years under the constitution: "It was generally assumed that if you were born in the Red Lake Hospital, built in 1914, you were a Red Laker. You've got to understand that in those days not many people left the reservation, and if you decided to leave, you were on your own."

By the late 1930s Indians were leaving the reservation with increasing frequency. During the war years hundreds of Red Lakers left: some joined the armed forces, many found wartime employment in the Twin Cities and other major cities throughout the nation. As a result, the "born-on-the-reservation" rule was challenged and a revision of the 1918 constitution permitted children born to Red Lake parents, regardless of their birthplace, to become members. In 1961 the Tribal Council amended the membership rule of the constitution to require a minimum of one-fourth Red Lake Indian blood.

Statistics give only one dimension. It is from the faces of the people that one should read to seek understanding: faces lined with age and care, alive with youthful mirth, caught in moments of repose and of action.

Yolanda French (front) and Janet Crowe at the Ponemah grade school

Madeline Benaise of Little Rock, well known before her death as a weaver of baskets in the traditional manner, now a forgotten art

The Rainclouds of Ponemah. Dan, born in 1903, is the recognized shaman of the reservation (spiritual leader or medicine man of the Midewiwin, the "Grand Medicine Society"). Madeline, born in 1889, is said to be one of the few living members of the Midewiwin to have participated in ceremonies of the eighth or highest degree.

*Nodin, Jr., born in 1875, was the "old man" or number one shaman
for many years in the Ponemah area. He now lives in a rest home off the reservation
and has delegated his position as spiritual leader to Dan Raincloud.*

Fanny Wind of Ponemah, born in 1887, with her granddaughter Ida Black

Henry Benaise of Little Rock, who died in 1971

Eugene Stillday, Jr., in Ponemah

The secretary in the Tribal Council office, Eloise White

Mrs. John (Maggie) Greenleaf, born in 1876

Ben Lawrence of Redlake. The buildings in the background represent three main periods of housing on the reservation: the log building, the tar-paper shack, and the modern "CAP" (Community Action Program) or prebuilt home.

Mr. and Mrs. John Fairbanks with the 38-star flag presented to a Red Lake hereditary chief as a good-will gesture by the president of the United States sometime between 1876 and 1889 — probably during the Treaty and Agreement of 1889. The home in the background is a good example of the tar-paper shack.

Raymond Cloud of Ponemah

*Allen Kingbird, Sr., almost a legend for
his skills as a hunter and trapper*

Mark and Vernon Kingbird, young Ponemah singers

*Andrew Sigana
of Ponemah*

51

The Water and the Woods

"There is no place better than the Indian reservation. It's so beautiful, the land is covered with dark green pine trees and other kinds of trees. At dawn we can watch the sun, and we will see the beautiful colors around the sun. We are proud of our reservation and we thank God for giving it to us."

Roland Lussier
Grade 6, St. Mary's Mission
School, 1973

"I like to play in the woods because I like the smile of the trees and brush. And I like the smile of the wind that goes by me."

Byron Lussier
Grade 5, St. Mary's Mission
School, 1973

"I like the sky at night because sometimes the Northern Lights dance at night and sometimes it is a good night out and I like to sit and look at the sky."

Shelly May
Grade 4, St. Mary's Mission
School, 1973

"My hair is black,
My skin is brown,
I'm an Indian.
I help take care of mother nature
*   and our beautiful resources.*
I'm an Indian
Of which I am proud
To be an Indian.
As I look over our land and lakes,
I thank God many times for this
*   wonderful place."*

Pamela May
Grade 6, St. Mary's Mission
School, 1973

THE WATER AND THE WOODS

The Martins, Kingbirds, Johnsons, Siganas, Frenchs, Clouds, and other fishermen of Ponemah and Redlake are a sturdy, weather-wise breed of men. Their fingers and palms are split and calloused, their forearms developed and hardened from pulling a half mile or more of net line twenty inches at a time. Their eyes are uncannily sharp: they have developed the ability to spot a small torn wisp of flag flying from a net marker pole in the early gray of dawn, where others see only whitecaps. They can move with a catlike balance and agility in a tossing metal boat filled with nets and wooden fish boxes. Like other men who live and work close to the water, they seem to have a deep, almost religious feeling for nature. Although they now cross the lake in aluminum boats pushed by forty-horsepower motors, and their nets are machine woven from synthetic fiber, the activity of setting and pulling a net has not changed for a hundred years. Fishing is still a way of life, a challenge, and in a very quiet manner competitive.

Almost daily during the months of July and August, while the sun is still cool and the grass wet, the fish-heavy nets are transported, usually in the trunk of a trail-battered sedan called "the fish car," to fish camps near the village. Here, in the shade of the hardwoods, the older members of the family clean the fish taken from the three-hundred-foot gill nets, sorting them into ice-filled boxes. Children, just tall enough to reach the cross rods of the drying poles, expertly untangle the nylon fibers, hanging the plastic floats on one end, the lead sinkers on the other. Although some families haul their own catch to the fishery each day, most rely on the daily run of fish trucks. For more than a quarter century George Pemberton and his sons have transported boxes of iced fish between Ponemah and the fishery in Redby, where they are filleted, scaled, and shipped by semitrailers to the markets of Minneapolis and Chicago.

If a man sets his nets in the evening he must pull them early the next morning. Only in the late fall and winter are the nets allowed to remain in the water for more than a day. If the nets are not pulled, the warm summer water and air temperatures will cause the fish to turn white and become "soft," unacceptable for market. To save the fish a man is often forced to cross six or more miles of rough white-water and struggle for hours in a pitching, rolling boat, pulling his heavy nets in a strong crosswind. During the last days of late fall fishing there is the risk of "icing over." A sudden drop in temperature and a windless night can trap two hundred dollars' worth of gill nets under the ice.

I have watched with admiration and affection these men who match wits and muscles with the elements. A fisherman of forty years' experience still pauses to gaze at the ever-changing beauty of sky and water, to throw small fish to the hovering gulls, and to laugh with excitement over a large catch. A man never boasts of a large catch. But his success does not go unnoticed and his skill as a fisherman and the size of his catch will be known to all the families in the village by the time his nets are dry.

During the long August afternoons men gather in the shade and talk about the morning catch and where they will set the nets tomorrow. And they remember and talk about another day in August, when a man caught 1000 pike, a day when he made three trips to gather his nets. Each day a man hopes he will become part of the legend.

Many of these same men spend part of the winter working in the woods cutting cedar in the swamps along the North Shore Trail, accessible only during the coldest months when the ground is frozen. They pull the logs out of the swamps on horse-drawn sleds, then haul them to the cedar fence plant in Redby in pickup trucks or trailers.

Here in the north country the winter days are short, six hours of daylight between sunrise and sunset. The average minimum temperature is zero or below every day from mid-December to March. It is not uncommon in January and February to have sustained periods of temperatures 30° below zero. The temperature can fluctuate sixty degrees in twelve hours, dropping from 20° at noon to −40° at midnight. These men can call the temperature within a few degrees by the sound of their boots on the frozen snow or the sharp cracking noises of wood splitting. In a few minutes the wind can whip a man's face to a painful red and split his lips, freezing tears to eyelashes. A few minutes without gloves, the time it takes to tighten a chain on a saw or adjust a carburetor, become a painful experience. When the temperature drops below −30°, wagon tongues and metal gears may crack under working loads. To these men who live north of 46 degrees latitude, wind direction is more important than the mathematics of a chill factor. A sudden shift of wind to the south and a rise in temperature, observed by one who has spent a lifetime looking into northern skies, quickly prompt a change in tomorrow's working schedule. The expression "square wheels" is not a cold-weather joke. When the temperature drops below −15°, nylon tires freeze in the parked position.

And for the first few hundred feet one is driving on square wheels.

Often the sunrise is marked with small rainbows of "diamond dust" created by the suspension of minute ice crystals in the air. And on some mornings the frost mist will cover the land like a fog.

Loggers heat their midday meal by warming coffee and toasting sandwiches over an open fire. Even on the severest days they seem to be indifferent to the cold and a comment about the weather will usually be answered with the polite and casual response, "It's just right for working in the woods."

Although a man may still choose to support his family by fishing or working in the woods, the once-common seasonal activities of gathering maple sugar, drying berries and fruits, and preparing meats have in part been replaced by the monthly distribution of United States Department of Agriculture surplus food commodities, the home freezer, and weekly trips to the supermarkets in Bemidji. At the same time hunting and fishing as avocations are still popular and continue to provide a significant part of the food supply for many families. Within the boundaries of the reservation a member of the Red Lake Band can hunt and fish without restrictions. Most of the hunting takes place from mid-summer to December. According to recent herd counts there are some 8000 deer within the reservation boundaries, a smaller moose herd, and an abundance of small game. Each fall an estimated half million ducks feed on the rice in the large western marshes.

Many Red Lakers still tan and soften their own animal hides, using the finished product to make moccasins and elaborate costumes for dancing. But this is for the most part an activity for weekends and after work. Hunting is usually done by "shining" — hunting at night and in the early hours of the morning by the beam of a spotlight. The hunter may stand on a wooden platform mounted on the top of a car or the back of a pickup. Some have modified farm tractors and built swamp buggies that make it possible to travel off the roads and trails into the marshes and brush. When men talk of hunting they mention places like "Ditch 30," "the old farm road," "the outlet," and the Mahnomen (Rice) River.

The Mahnomen River area is a place that can still challenge the imagination of the adventurer. An area without roads or trails and accessible only by crossing the lake, it is true wilderness. In the late summer a few Ponemah families travel up the river — red in color from mineral deposits — to gather wild rice, poling through the marshes (even as their grandparents did) and beating the rice grains into the small ricing boats with long sticks. A few men visit the area each year to hunt or trap; they tell of seeing beaver colonies, large timber wolves, and moose. The stretch of wilderness beach from the Narrows to the mouth of the river abounds with wildlife and is one of the most beautiful and isolated areas of the reservation.

A summer storm over Red Lake (looking west from the Blackduck River bridge)

Fishermen Albert ("Binger") King and Bobby Head riding out a squall

Joe Barrett and Paul ("Snuffy") Smith setting nets (each is about a hundred yards long)

Rufus Johnson and son pulling gill nets at sunrise

Isaac Kingbird, Jr., with his catch, mostly whitefish

Returning fishermen in rough weather

The Sigana family cleaning whitefish at Ponemah

Nets and fishboxes are often transported from home to shore in an older car called "the fish car." This same trail-battered vehicle is used to carry the hunter and the logger over the back country.

*The "fish camp" is often a shady area near the home. Here the fish
are taken from the miles of gill nets and packed in ice.*

*Smoking whitefish over an open fire
at the Isaac Kingbird home, Ponemah*

Hanging nets for drying is a daily chore during the summer months

Fishermen returning at dusk after setting nets

Winter fishing, when the temperature may drop to −20° or colder.
Nets are pulled about twice a week in winter. Long poles and string are used
to set new nets through holes in the ice.

Charles Cloud and Allen Kingbird, Sr.,
returning to their car after
checking traps at Ponemah

71

Joe Barrett chopping a hole at the base of a muskrat house to check a trap. He is one of the few men who make their winter income on a trap line. The Ki Wo Say wildlife area and the large marsh areas along the Clearwater River abound with muskrat, mink, and wolves.

Vernon Clark and John G. Smith of Redby dressing a moose killed by Clark the night before on the west end

During late August and September moose hunters drive along the fifteen-mile strip of highway 1 on the west end of the reservation scanning the open grasslands and cedar swamps in the first light of day

Keith Defoe and Francis Downwind of Redby, who had killed two deer and their first moose while shining on an August night

Frank Hill of Redlake, dressing an early morning kill on the lakeshore

*Mr. and Mrs. Charles Anderson of Redlake ricing on Fourth Lake. She is
"beating the rice" (knocking the ripe grains into the boat);
he is poling the narrow, flat-bottom ricing boat.*

The Beat of the Drum

"It's going to be a nice peaceful day when I make my sound."

From "Song of the Eagle"

"Come to the Red Lake Reservation.
If you want to see a celebration,
Come on over.
You can see beautiful costumes
On the Fourth of July.
You can even try to dance yourself;
Come on, try a few steps.
I am telling you,
You will love it.
If you come bring some friends,
All kinds of them.
You can even make some new ones."

Marilyn May
Grade 8, St. Mary's Mission
School, 1973

THE BEAT OF THE DRUM

Among the community activities of the Red Lakers no other, perhaps, symbolizes traditional "Indianness" as much as the pow-wow. A powwow is a ceremony which combines the talent and skill of the singer-drummer and of the dancer. The occasion may be the annual Fourth of July celebration, a four-day event that has been held near the village of Redlake each year for almost a half century (Ponemah also has its Fourth of July fete). It is the social highlight of the summer, a time when hundreds of relatives and visitors return to the reservation. The sound of the drum may also be part of a program to celebrate the dedication of a new building, or a ceremony to honor a young man going into the army. Singing may be a spontaneous reaction to mood and feeling, a recalling of another time and place. I have seen this happen on a quiet August night when four singers placed a large drum on the sandy shore of Ponemah Point. Silhouetted against the last light of day, they bent to the heavy beat of the fur-tipped sticks, the clear singsong wail of the singers rising through the air — a sound that has not changed for thousands of sunsets. The present became the past.

Over a period of a lifetime a man will learn many songs, some passed on from generation to generation, others new with the season — the "Song of the Eagle," the "Air Corps Song," the "Friendship Song," the "Flag Song," the "Gift Giving Song." (Today the sounds are recorded on hundreds of pop-up, flip-over tape cassettes, but these only crudely suggest the scene.) To "sing" is to bring forth a sound that is shaped by a hundred small manipulations of the vocal cords, mouth, tongue, and lips. It is a unique sound. It is an Indian sound. Not all Indian men are singers, however, and not all singers are great singers.

It is natural for a father to encourage his sons to become singers. A small boy may grow up standing at the edge of the drum circle. A circle of three or more intense, somber, sweating men. Sometimes echoing, sometimes reinforcing the sound of the leader. One hand holds the drumstick, the other forms a cup between mouth and ear to amplify the voice. The eyes stare, but appear not to see, giving the impression that all available sensory strength is being used by the voice. Occasionally the singer will turn from the drum and spit the phlegm from his throat. The men are always serious. There are times, in the afternoon or early in the evening, when a young boy may be permitted to kneel between the men and beat on the metal edge of the drum with a stick. Then one day, when it is time, he will have the courage and the confidence to drum on the white surface, straighten his body, lean forward, and make the sound. It is time to become a man.

Loring Sumner collecting gifts to be distributed to those taking part in the annual Fourth of July powwow, a practice discontinued about 1969

A planned powwow is a celebration, a competition, a spectator event, and is advertised by poster. It is scheduled to begin at a definite hour. But the dancers and drummers will enter the fenced ring of the powwow circle at a special time called "Indian time." It is a combination of weather, temperature, digestive systems, events of the past night, mood, enthusiasm, and countless other factors. Briefly: the powwow will begin when the time is right.

Although there may be some dancing in midday, Red Lake powwows normally begin sometime in the evening. At sunset the drummers sing the "Flag Song," and the flag above the drum shelter is lowered and folded with respect by war veterans. The pace begins slowly. A few young dancers begin to circle in a sun-wise direction. The young men enter and begin to circle. They are the fancy dancers. Their feathered bustles flash in the light and their deer-hair headpieces respond to vibrations of the body. They move rapidly between the women and the traditional dancers like birds in flight, touching the ground lightly, twice between drum beats. Their costumes represent uncounted winter hours of beadwork. At midnight the ring lights glow on the blurred movement of a hundred dancers.

There are some, like Ethel Johnson in Ponemah, who feel the earlier significance of the powwow is being lost in the competitiveness characterizing the "summer powwow circuit." (From Memorial Day to Labor Day, every weekend finds the drummers, singers, and dancers leaving to compete for prize money at scheduled performances throughout the land of the Chippewa and Sioux nations.) But there are still times in Ponemah when the sound of the drum and the chant of the singers have a religious meaning and a small gathering of friends will still observe the traditional sharing of food and the passing of ceremonial tobacco as part of the powwow.

The flag ceremony as evening powwow events are about to begin when the flag
is carried around the powwow ring, the singers play the ''Veterans' Song,'' and veterans
are invited to walk around the circle. During this 1969 ceremony
the flag is carried by Kenneth Stately (''Buddy Bosh''), left, and Sam Yankee,
then chief of the Mille Lacs Chippewa Band.

The flag-lowering ceremony in 1973

A visiting Sioux drum from the Dakotas at the Fourth of July powwow in 1969

Red Lake women playing cards during the afternoon at the powwow campground

Alex Whitefeather, Pete Seymour, and Ole Johnson during an informal afternoon drum session at the campground

Powwow singers. To amplify the sound of his voice and to isolate the voice from the sound of the drums, a man cups his hand from mouth to ear.

Dancers circling the drummers in a sunwise direction

*Leonard Stately, Jr. ("Robin"),
and Della White*

Informal or open dancing during the afternoon of the Fourth of July powwow in 1964

Kenneth Stately ("Buddy Bosh") recording songs at a powwow

A visiting dancer getting ready for evening competition in 1964

The Road to Ponemah

"God! I beg You to listen to what I am going to say.

"In our Indian way we always give You cigarettes and the eats. I want you to share these things with Your sons and the servants You have in Your kingdom; also the Thunderbirds. We know You hear every one of us when we speak to You. We also know that when we use our minds You know us right away. God, I am asking You to let us live to remember this day next year again, both old and children. I am thankful for this building that they have made for us. I sure am thankful in every way."

Translation of a prayer given
in Chippewa by Dan Raincloud at the
dedication of the new fire station
and office building in Ponemah,
on August 30, 1972

"We have our race of Indians. Our culture. The land around us. When I think of it, we have something that no one else can make but God. You would have to be an Indian to understand what I'm saying. I just can't describe it. Sometimes I wish we'd still live in the old way. You could walk anywhere without being disturbed. When I go into the woods it's like taking a trip to heaven. But when I come out of the woods, I see the white man's way. And, sometimes, I forget my Indian way. We Indians of the reservation don't want to forget our race. Today many people are drowning out our race. That's why I say we have some-thing that others don't."

Julie Oliver
Grade 6, St. Mary's
Mission School, 1973

THE ROAD TO PONEMAH

Five miles east of Redby the main road of the reservation makes a ninety-degree turn north and is called the road to Ponemah. Travel the road north, through Mahquam Bay where the great bald eagles still hover over the tall pines, cross the deep black waters of the Blackduck and Battle rivers where the great chiefs and warriors held councils, and continue to where the road touches the lake at the Narrows. This is the road to Ponemah — and also the road to the past. Until 1901 the village was called Cross Lake. When an application for a post office was filed in 1901 the name Ponemah was selected. In translation it means ''hereafter'' or ''a little later.'' Historically ''progress'' has always been a little slow to find its way to Ponemah.

When an attempt was made in 1900 to build a boarding school in the area called O-bash-ing (''a place where the wind blows through''), the traditional site of an early burial ground and village, the Indians resisted and demanded that the school be built farther east, where the present village is located. Because of their continued desire to protect a way of life they understand, the 140 families from Mahquam Bay to Ponemah Point have over the years been less than enthusiastic in welcoming any effort by outsiders to introduce change. As a result the ''Indian way of doing things'' has been better preserved in Ponemah than elsewhere on the reservation.

The people here are clannish; there is less intermarriage with nonmembers or outsiders. The residents of Ponemah are a ''family.'' Together they help carry a man's sadness and together they celebrate a time of joy. Ponemah is the home of the Clouds, Whitefeathers, Rainclouds, Rosebears, Johnsons, Stilldays, and the Iceman family. Members of the Kingbird family have been living on the quarter-mile road leading to the Narrows as long as most people can remember.

Ponemah residents, like other Red Lakers, watch the Minnesota Vikings on television and gather at the community center to play

Bingo on Tuesday nights; they own automobiles and build frame houses. But they also still smoke whitefish and goldeye over open fires and cross North Lake to the backwaters of the Mahnomen River to hunt and to harvest wild rice in the immemorial way. A man in Ponemah is still given his Indian name, and here people over thirty speak in Chippewa as often as they do in English. A Ponemah little-league coach is likely to shout, "Mahjuhn, mahjuhn!" (Go) to the boy leading off third base.

There are people living in the village of Redlake who have never taken the forty-minute ride to Ponemah. It is ironic that many young students — Indian and white — attending Bemidji State College are enrolled in courses called "Indian Studies" yet have never been to Ponemah to talk with the older people about the Indian way.

Over the past half century much of that way, even in Ponemah, has disappeared — forever. Some of the old has been preserved, copied, catalogued, some say saved, by scholars. And there are efforts to draw on the riches stored in the memories of the Ponemah elders. Dan Raincloud, one of the last shamans or "priests" of the Midewiwin (called by whites the Grand Medicine Society), is for instance invited to the University of Minnesota once a year to give a short lecture on the old way. But the passing of every old man or woman results in the loss of some tradition, some link with the past. Ten years ago, there were several men at Red Lake who were recognized as shamans of the Indian religion. Today, besides Dan Raincloud, there is only Nodin, Jr., ninety-eight years old, who lives in the rest home; he is still in good health and often attends ceremonies in Ponemah, but he has delegated his responsibilities to Dan.

Although it is not the custom to look too far into the future, Dan has begun to talk about the course of the Midewiwin in Ponemah during coming years. At his sixty-eighth birthday party, I asked him what would happen to the Indian religion in Ponemah if he were not there. "Perhaps," he smiled, "Reverend Hayes will have to take over." (The Reverend Mr. Hayes is the minister of the Northern Gospel Mission, first established on the reservation in 1928. In 1954 this Christian mission obtained permission from the Tribal Council to use a piece of land for erecting a permanent building in Ponemah. The Wah-Bun — or Morning — Chapel serves the community with a light evangelistic appeal and a lot of community service. Inside the mission are several coin-operated washing machines, a television set, and a soft-drink machine. Although services are held regularly, the biggest gatherings take place outside at the hot and cold water faucets and under the basketball hoop nailed to the front of the mission.) It is more likely, however, that one of the Ponemah adults who have been listening to the "old men" and who are fourth-degree Mide will be asked to sit closer to Dan in the future and to share in the sacred words and practices of the Midewiwin. (There are eight degrees or lodges in Midewiwin, but only in exceptional cases does a candidate go beyond the fourth.)

Dan Raincloud has devoted half of his more than three-score years talking to the "old men," learning the words, medicines, and practices of the Indian religion. Myths and the legendary history of the

Chippewa are an important part of the Midewiwin ceremonies — as they were in the nineteenth century when William W. Warren recorded the old priest's narrative of the early travels of the tribe. Time and individual interpretations have produced numerous variations in these traditions, which are passed on orally from one generation to another. Where Dan uses the word "God," others have used the expression "Great Spirit." When I asked Dan if God and Nanabojo were the same spirit and if they created the same world, he explained, "Nanabojo is God's brother. God created the world below, underneath. Nanabojo created the world on top according to legend. The first world was covered by a great flood after a conflict between Nanabojo and the evil underwater spirits. The 'new earth' created by Nanabojo was made for the Indian."

When events take place in a manner associated with an earlier time they are said to happen "Indian fashion," "Indian custom," or "in the old way." Today, the casual reference to an event that will take place in the old way usually refers to a burial service in Ponemah conducted in the tradition of the Midewiwin. It is common to read in the weekly *Redlake Neighborhood Centers Newsletter* that funeral services will be held for a Ponemah resident "in the Indian custom."

Over the years the complex ceremonies of the Midewiwin have been altered and have become simplified as the result of changing life-styles and training of the recognized medicine men. I have found some confusion about whether the road of souls and the land of spirits lie to the east, west, or somewhere out in space. There is, however, a belief, related in stories as recent as World War II, that there is a separate heaven for the red man. It is said in Ponemah that the face of the deceased is painted with red circles so there will be no mistake in the hereafter and the person will be admitted to the Indian heaven. I have been told that the Midewiwin is not so much to worship anything as to give thanks to the Mide Manito (grand medicine spirit), to ask for special favors from the Great Spirit through the intercession of lesser spirits in the form of birds and animals called manito, and to preserve the knowledge of natural medicines (herbs, roots, bark) and practices used to cure illness and prolong life. It is a religion that is concerned with relationships between people. Although I've heard older people talk of evil spirits that can cause illness and misfortune, the concept of a devil and a hell appears not to be part of Midewiwin beliefs.

After dinner one summer evening, I asked a resident of Ponemah who is a member of the Gospel Mission if he was a Christian. His reply expressed a cover-all-bases philosophy on religion: "Well, why take a chance? Maybe their way is right." He's also an adherent of the Indian religious way. "Because maybe the Indian way is right and there is a separate heaven for the red man."

One March night in Ponemah Dan honored me by relating part of the story of the creation of the Indian world as it had been passed on to him through the Midewiwin. He has given me permission to reproduce it here. (The story of the creation of the Indian world is used in the Midewiwin burial rite. As Dan warned, "These are the words we use when somebody dies. Half of it, it's not dangerous, and half of it, it's dangerous.'' There is a fear that if the second part is told — out of the context of the ceremony — someone could die.)

"When God came to this world, there was no white man, no Indian. He looked around the sky and he looked at the world and he made up his mind what he was going to do. He picked up the ground and placed it behind him. When he brought it in front of him, there was a woman, an Indian. He told this woman, 'I'm placing you here to live.' Again he did the same thing. He grabbed the ground, placed it behind him, and when he opened his hand, there was an animal with four legs. He placed him here on the ground and told the animal, 'This is an Indian, you call her an Indian and she'll call you Great Spirit (manito). But you got to take care of this Indian and she got to take care of you as well.' He did this four times and made the lion, bear, wolf, and fox. He again did the same thing — four times — and created the birds — golden eagle, two thunderbirds, and all the other big birds, like the condores, and he told each one, 'I'm going to put you in the heaven so you can watch the Indian here, and she'll watch you as well. You call her anishinabe — an Indian — and she'll call you manito.'

"When he got through he talked to what he had made, talked to the woman; and the woman thanked God. And he went on to tell these manito: 'Make more! make more, as up in heaven. And when you get through, you come and tell me.' When they got through, this manito — whoever it is, his name is never mentioned, but this 'short-armed' manito [otter], that's what we call him, he could go anywheres — he was sent to tell God everything was all done.

" 'All right,' God said, 'now the next thing you got to do is make another Indian for that woman to stay with.' So these manito gathered around and looked for a way to make another Indian. While the woman was sleeping, one of these manito took one of her ribs and made a man. When the woman woke she was told that God wanted her to have a husband.

"One day God, who was watching these Indians and what they were doing, came down again and appeared before the Indians and he gave them grain, like the white man raises, and written matter. These two things he gave the Indian and, because everywhere he looked he saw deer, moose, bear, God gave him a bow and arrow but said, 'I'm giving you this, but you are to use it only when you are hungry and want to eat something.'

"Then God went back again. He was watching the Indian. All this time, the only thing the Indian was doing was hunting with his bow and arrow. He didn't care about the grain and the written matter so God got tired watching him and said, 'Now look here, didn't I give you written matter and grain to plant? I'm going to take the grain away and also the written matter.' But God put his hand on top of the Indian's head and said, 'Anything that happened way back you still will remember it but I'm taking away the seeds. You're going to make yourself sweat because you are going to work hard.' The Indian didn't say anything. He knew he was making a mistake. [The Indian had chosen the life of the hunter and rejected farming.]

"God left again and all these manito gathered and somebody spoke up and asked, 'Are the Indians going to have a religion?' Somebody said, 'Yes.' So one of them was hired to go after the first Indian [sometimes called Cutfoot]. When the Indian got there with the manito he saw four old men, old men with white hair. He was asked to sit down and one of them said, 'We're going to tell you what your religion will be — Midewiwin. That's what we are going to give you, but be sure to catch on to it.' And the four old men began to tell him about Midewiwin. Four times they called for him, and taught him how to do his religion. When they finished one of these older men said, 'Who made this world? We should ask him to listen when this Indian does his religion. He's got to ask, who made this world?' So this, the one I was talking about, the 'short-arm, strong-arm' [otter] we call him, he was sent over there to God again. He went to God and he said, 'God, I'm sent here to come and ask you if you can come over there [earth]. Manito wants to talk to you.' So God came down again and he was asked, 'Did you make this world for this Indian?' God said, 'No! The one I made is, it's under! It's under! But the top one here, I didn't make that. You go ask Nanabojo. He might be the man that made this world on top of what I made under.' So this 'strong-arm, short-arm' again he was sent; he knew where Nanabojo was. So Nanabojo came here and he was told to sit down with the other manito and the Indian as well. But this time the Indian woman came along. She too listened to what was said. Nanabojo said, 'You are welcome to use my land.' And right away he made this pipe and plate, for he thought he would be the first one to be talked about when the Indian wanted to do Midewiwin. He'd be the first one to be talked about and to get tobacco, mideassema we call it, and the eats, midewesinni [offering to an honored guest]. And he watched the Indian.

"When the Indian had children he was told, 'Anytime your child is sick, go to Midewiwin and he'll get well or she'll get well.' And he went on to do this. Well, Nanabojo was a son-of-a-gun, he was listening. This Indian started with his Midewiwin. Nanabojo put his pipe here and his plate. He knew that tobacco would be put into his pipe and the eats on his plate. The Indian started out, never a word about him, and then quit. Well, Nanabojo just put up his pipe here beside him and the plate. He didn't get mad right away. He was wondering when the Indian would go at it again. Again he heard the Indian starting his Midewiwin. Once more he put his pipe and plate in front of him. All this time the Indian never mentioned anything about Nanabojo. Well, his Grand Medicine Dance was all over and again Nanabojo put his pipe and plate away. Twice the Indian had forgotten to talk about Nanabojo. The third time the Indian did his Midewiwin, Nanabojo said, 'I suppose that this time the Indian will talk about me first, because I'm the one that made this world.'

"The Indian started again and all the way through he never mentioned Nanabojo. Nanabojo threw his pipe and plate backwards. He got mad. He stood up and pointed to where the Indian was. 'You Indian, I'll still find where I can grab a mideassema and midewesinni' — these are what he was waiting for. So that's where the Indian started and that's only part of the story. But the rest of it is dangerous."

The post office and center of the village of Ponemah. Buildings in the background were stores vacated in the 1950s. They were leveled in 1972.

Waiting for mail to be sorted at the post office in Ponemah

A historic day: the first pre-constructed home to cross the Battle River en route to Ponemah, July 1972. Houses are built at an assembly site in Redby next to the Indian Mills.

The road to Ponemah. The blacktop has many uses — children write on it, play and ride bikes on it, often lie on the warm surface to dry their clothes after swimming.

Recess for grade school girls and boys at Ponemah

Swimming among the rushes behind Jimmy Cloud's house in Ponemah. Red Lake is a perfect lake for young swimmers with its sandy shallow shoreline. It's often possible to walk one hundred yards or so to a depth of five feet.

A child's hammock made from a folded blanket — a technique so common it is often used in the Red Lake hospital. There are no baby cribs in Ponemah. The hammock is efficient, safe, and wastes no floor space.

Harlan Kingbird and Carol Kingbird
of Ponemah on a summer evening

Mrs. Perry White and her baby, with parents Joe
and Nellie Dick in the background, in 1973

The Rudy Kingbird family of Ponemah in 1973

Eugene and Alfreda Stillday and family
on a summer cookout

Ella Kingbird and the Headstart class at the Ponemah community center

High school students after classes at the community center

The Ponemah volunteer fire department in a training session. The community center and new fire station and office buildings are in the background.

Wake and burial for Robert Iceman, summer 1969. This was perhaps the last Red Lake burial ceremony to take place in a home; today wakes and services are commonly held in the community center. The wake usually takes place the day and evening after death. The wake is a quiet vigil, with ceremonial prayers offered by the medicine man in the Midewiwin tradition. On the afternoon of the burial there is a feast. Traditionally the men eat first, then the women. Each guest fills his plate and offers a portion of everything he takes, including tobacco, to the spirit of the deceased. After the feast there are ceremonial prayers and the coffin is transported to the family burial ground. When the ceremony took place in the home, the body was removed from the south or west window — I have been told this was

continued on page 116

continued from page 114

done so that the spirit of the deceased could set out for the land of spirits in the right direction and so that the spirit did not "touch" the living. As a veteran of World War II Robert Iceman was buried with military honors. Members of the Bemidji American Legion post officiated and presented the flag to Mrs. Iceman.

A grave house or spirit house, common in the Ponemah area where traditional Midewiwin customs are still observed. The addition of a marker like those used for Christian graves reflects the compromise that often is made between the old way and the modern.

A gathering of friends and relatives in Ponemah to honor a young man leaving for army service, Alvin Still-day. Dan Raincloud offered ceremonial tobacco before the feast.

118

There are two annual powwows in Ponemah — the Fourth of July and Labor Day.
Each is at least a two-day affair, a time for the community to gather, with many guests
coming from Canadian communities, especially the Whitefish Bay area of Ontario.

A meeting of friends at Murial Rosebear's in Ponemah, with "give-away blankets"
hanging from the line, with the passing of ceremonial tobacco, and with
words of offering spoken by the "old men" before the feast. There are still
times in the Ponemah area when the traditional concept of the drum and
the dance, with religious and other ceremonial overtones, is still preserved.

Drummer-singers on the shore of Red Lake at the Narrows

Ke-Go-Way-Se-Kah

"After camping out four nights, and traveling each day through a prairie country, the soul arrives in the land of spirits, where he finds his relatives accumulated since mankind was first created; all is rejoicing, singing and dancing; they live in a beautiful country interspersed with clear lakes and streams, forests and prairies, and fruit and game — in a word, all which conduces most to his happiness."

William W. Warren, in
History of the Ojibway Nation, 1853

*"I'm gonna go; as far as I can
I have to go; seems I can't find it,
I have to look; as far as I can
Gotta look and look, until I find it.
If I find it, I'll stop going.
I need help to get started
Need help to go
Maybe I'll ask someone or something
I'll try hard and I'll go.
Gotta keep looking, until I find ME!"*

Deanna Lasley, Sophomore,
Red Lake High School, 1973

KE-GO-WAY-SE-KAH

Ke-go-way-se-kah — you are going homeward. Traditionally this has meant the route of souls after death to the "beautiful country interspersed with clear lakes and streams, forests and prairies, and fruit and game," where the Indian can find, in Warren's glowing words, "all which conduces most to his happiness."

For those at Red Lake a beautiful country with clear lakes and streams and green forests, with fruit and fish and game, where they may dance and sing at will, is already a reality. And for some this is enough in the here and now. But life in the mundane world of today encompasses for most Red Lakers other elements as the individual searches for earthly happiness — or, perhaps better, for self-fulfillment, for "me." The Red Laker, however often and naturally he may take a step into the past (beating a drum ceremonially; alone in the woods among aged trees; working a traditional beadwork pattern), is surrounded by the present and the things and ideas of the white man's society.

His children — reared to value one culture — go to schools very like those of white communities so that they may understand and share, if they wish, another culture. This is not easy for them. As the counselor at Red Lake high school, John Ward, put it, "We realize that many of the young people are caught between two cultures and are struggling to find a compromise." Restless youngsters at Red Lake find release for their energies in rock music — like their white contemporaries — as often as they do in the dance of the powwow.

For the diseases and other ailments of the body, the Red Laker may turn to the herb panaceas of his forebears; he is more likely to rely on the modern health care of the professionally trained doctors and dentists on the reservation. (But some may prudently decide to take no chances — and hang medicine bags beside their doors.)

Past, present — and future: Red Lakers, as I see them, cherish the past, live in sometimes uneasy, sometimes serene equilibrium with the present, face the uncertain future with the same mixture of exhilaration and foreboding as the rest of us. But I do not want to generalize unduly. To me, the Red Lakers stand tall and free. That is enough to say.

On a hot August afternoon young Red Lakers gather at the Mud Creek bridge on highway 1, near the Red Lake fishery in Redby

High school students in 1969

A practice session by members of "The Tribe,"
Terry Adams, drummer, and J. R. Rouse

Diana Skinaway of Redlake watching girls' slow pitch action

Janet Graves talking to friends before a movie at Redlake

The recreational hall at Redlake in the winter of 1969.
The building is now the United States post office.

Redby youths with their portable record player

Rufus Johnson of Ponemah
demonstrating his technique
with the bow at
a day camp

*Two Red Lake ladies' slow
pitch teams in action*

Lavern Donnell, a member of the Red Lake men's hardball team

High school basketball, Red Lake versus Cass Lake

135

*Sister Louise and her students
at St. Mary's Mission School*

Teacher Mary Moret and first graders at the Ponemah school

Roxanne Strong in catechism class at St. Mary's Mission School

Jeffrey Iceman at the Ponemah grade school

Peter Neadeau, Jr., in an art class at the high school

Raymond Strong in a math class at the high school

Duane Beck, teacher, with student Marlyce Morrison in an accounting class

Phyllis ("Jetto") Johnson in a sewing class at the high school

Randy Kingbird and classmates at the Ponemah grade school

In a shop class at the high school
Janet Schoenborn develops welding skills

Teacher Lorena Cook and student Williamette
Hardy working on secretarial skills
at the vocational school

Mechanics class at the vocational school

Karen Holstein typing copy for the Redlake Neighborhood Centers Newsletter

Policewoman

Coffee break and time to discuss the 1974 model cars. Fabian Dudley, left, and Leo Desjarlait at the Red Lake Indian Mill.

Mill worker Larry Roy

The laundromat at Redlake

Bingo night at the Ponemah community center

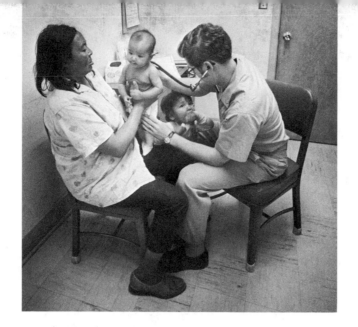

At the Red Lake hospital

*A child being measured during his monthly checkup
at the Red Lake hospital baby clinic*